FUN WITH GROWING THINGS

JOAN ECKSTEIN and JOYCE GLEIT have written seven books for children together. They have been friends for almost all of their lives, and their children are also friends.

Joan Eckstein divides her time between her farm in Massachusetts and her apartment in Brooklyn Heights. She is a gourmet cook, a gardener, and also an artist.

Joyce Gleit lives in a house in a suburb of New York City. She grows flowers and veggies in her backyard, takes in stray kittens, and collects jokes for kids from every corner of the country.

FUN WITH GROWING THINGS

JOAN ECKSTEIN and JOYCE GLEIT

Illustrations by Mena Dolobowsky

Revised Edition

AN AVON CAMELOT BOOK

To:
Paul, Jonathan, Lisa, Stefanie
Our young garden specialists

Because the level of maturity and dexterity varies from child to child, adult guidance and close supervision are strongly recommended. No child should ever attempt to use tools, chemicals, insecticides, or sprays without first securing permission from an adult.

FUN WITH GROWING THINGS is an original publication of Avon Books.

AVON BOOKS
A division of
The Hearst Corporation
105 Madison Avenue
New York, New York 10016

Text copyright © 1975, 1991 by Joan Eckstein and Joyce Gleit
Text illustrations copyright © 1991 by Avon Books
Published by arrangement with the authors
Library of Congress Catalog Card Number: 90-23021
ISBN: 0-380-76120-3
RL: 5.7

Library of Congress Cataloging in Publication Data:
Eckstein, Joan.
    Fun with growing things / Joan Eckstein and Joyce Gleit; illustrations by Mena Dolobowsky.—Rev. ed.
        p.   cm.—(Avon Camelot book)
    Summary: Presents step-by-step instructions for growing plants outdoors and indoors. Includes projects such as leaf printing and making a sponge garden and a scarecrow.
    1. Gardening—Juvenile literature. [1. Gardening.] I. Gleit, Joyce.
II. Dolobowsky, Mena, ill. III. Title.   90-23021
SB457.E23   1991   CIP
635—dc20   AC

Second Avon Camelot Edition, First Printing: March 1991

CAMELOT TRADEMARK REG. U.S. PAT. OFF. AND IN OTHER COUNTRIES, MARCA REGISTRADA, HECHO EN U.S.A.

Printed in the U.S.A.

OPM 10 9 8 7 6 5 4 3 2 1

CONTENTS

PART 2: GARDENING INDOORS

INTRODUCTION

Growing a garden of your own may seem like an impossible order at first. After all, how can you possibly make things grow in that clump of dirt covered over with weeds and rocks? Well, it really isn't as easy as a game of catch, but we promise it will be as much fun as playing. And the thrill of eating your own home-grown vegetables or picking your own flowers will be as exciting as the time you first learned to swim or catch a high-flying ball.

Gardening for kids can be a terrifically exciting experience. There is nothing to equal the joy of planting a seed and seeing that first sprout pushing through the earth.

If you're a city kid and only have a window ledge to call your own, we have a chapter on plants that can be grown in a window box and information on planting in pots. We have also included some odd and interesting things and ways to plant them. You can get as much enjoyment out of a few small plants that you nurtured yourself as the kid with a backyard garden. Some of you kids may be lucky enough to have a larger plot of ground to grow your own vegetables. For you there is the pleasure of picking your first crop and seeing it served at the dinner table.

Our suggestions and rules for growing a garden are simple and easy to follow, with a wide variety of suggestions, so that each individual kid can choose what is best for his surroundings. We have also included some fun projects for kids to try.

Read all instructions carefully and remember that each step is important in growing a healthy garden. You will be surprised at how much fun it is to churn up the earth, plant the seeds and water your garden. You will probably come out every morning eager to see if your seeds have come to life. And then there will be that one day when the first tiny sprout appears, and you will know that you did it all by yourself. You made something grow.

Be sure to get permission for the space and tools you are going to use for your garden. *Do not* use anything from the pantry or tool shed unless you get a grown-up's permission. *Do not* use chemicals or insecticides or sprays. *Always* let a grown-up know what you are doing and what you are using.

A LIST OF GARDEN HELPERS

Good creatures that are beneficial for your garden:

Insects:

dragonflies	eat harmful insects
spiders	eat harmful insects
praying mantis	eat harmful insects
wasps	eat beetles
ladybugs	eat aphids

Birds	eat harmful insects
Toads	eat insects
Bees	propagate
Butterflies	propagate

Earthworms

Earthworms are very good for the soil. Be glad when you see one. They help to grow healthy plants. Worms tunnel through the earth and help the soil to keep air, moisture, and calcium. You might want to raise earthworms to put into your garden. You probably can get them from your local nursery.

Insects are very strong creatures for their size. Ants and bees are especially strong. An ant can lift fifty times its own weight, and a bee can pull a load that is equivalent to a human pulling three big trailer trucks by himself.

The largest earthworms in the world are an Australian breed. They can measure two yards long when all curled up, and ten feet long when they are stretched out. They grow longer than some kinds of snakes.

Paul: *What are you doing there? Fishing?*
Jonathan: *No. I'm giving these worms a bath.*

A YOUNG GARDENER'S VOCABULARY

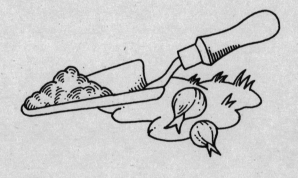

Annual A plant that completes its cycle in one season. It grows and does not come back the following season. Some examples are marigolds, zinnias, and sweet alyssums.

Biennial A plant which takes two growing seasons to complete its life cycle. The first season it grows roots and leaves, the next season it blooms. Examples are pansies, hollyhocks, and foxgloves.

Chlorophyll The green coloring in a plant. It is used by the plant to feed itself. Plants live on a mixture of water and carbon dioxide from the air, which the chlorophyll helps the plant to absorb. Humans live on water and oxygen in the air. We breathe in oxygen and breathe out the carbon dioxide, and plants do it the other way around. They take in carbon dioxide and give off oxygen. That is why it is so important to have a balance between plants and humans.

Compost heap A compost heap is made up of vegetable scraps and plant discards. When you pile all of these together, they begin to rot and blend together. You are making your own fertilizer. Compost is very good for your plants and vegetables. A compost heap may seem to you like a pile of garbage because it is composed of leftover food scraps, but it becomes a source of food for your plants.

Cultivate	There are two definitions for the word *cultivate*. One means to prepare the ground for planting by plowing or digging and fertilizing. You also *cultivate* the earth by digging around the roots of your plant with a garden tool called a cultivator. The word *cultivate* also means to nurture and grow something.
Drainage	The running off of water gradually from the earth where your plants are growing. Good drainage ensures nourishment to your plants but the water does not collect around your plants to drown them.
Fertilizer	This means extra nourishment for your plants. Air and water are essential for growth of plants. Sometimes the soil doesn't give enough other nourishment and then you have to add fertilizer. There are many kinds of fertilizer—natural kinds like animal manure or rotted organic material (compost heap stuff); or artificial chemical kinds. We recommend natural fertilizers. Buy fertilizer that is good for the soil in your area from your local nursery or garden supply store. The directions on the package will tell you how much to use for the size of your plot.
Flat	A shallow frame or box in which you plant seeds early to start them growing before transplanting them into your garden.
Germinate	To begin to grow or sprout.
Humus	Partially or totally decayed vegetable matter which is good food for plants and helps the soil to hold water.
Insecticide (Pesticide) (Fungicide)	Chemical substances used to rid a garden of insects and plant diseases. They are usually poisonous and therefore should be used with great care. They can be bought in a plant store or nursery. The directions for use are on the label.

10

We don't recommend using them, but if you think it is necessary to use any of these products *get the advice and help of an adult*. And remember, any plant or vegetable that has been sprayed must be washed very thoroughly and carefully before eating.

Mulch A protective covering of rotted organic material such as hay, old leaves, peat moss, wood chips, grass clippings, or pine needles, used to keep down weeds or protect the roots of your plants. Spread mulch around the roots of plants and loosen often with a rake or cultivator so that the mulch doesn't get too matted down.

Peat Moss A kind of moss that grows in very wet places. It is gathered and processed and then sold in nurseries and gardening stores. You buy it to use as mulch and plant food or mix it into the soil.

Perennial A plant that lives three or more seasons. In the autumn the stems die but the roots remain alive and the plant blooms again in the spring. Examples: daffodils, irises, roses, peonies, delphiniums.

Photosynthesis The process by which green plants (containing chlorophyll) convert light into energy and in doing so give off oxygen. This is why plants are so important to human and animal life. Without plants we would have no oxygen to breathe.

Pinch back To take off extra leaves and shoots that grow as your plant grows, so that your flowers, fruit, and plants can grow fuller and healthier. Do this especially with tomato plants as the tiny new shoots rob the plant of nourishment but don't produce any fruit.

11

Plant food	Sold in the plant store either in powder or liquid form. This is fertilizer for your plants and is used after your plants are in the ground. Follow directions on the package of whichever kind you buy.
Propagate	To cause plants to increase, spread, and multiply. Bees help do this when they fly from flower to flower by carrying pollen which fertilizes the plants.
Prune	To cut off dead branches or leaves to make room for healthy new growth in plants and trees.
Shoot	A young bud or leaf growing on a plant. The sprout that grows from the seed you have planted.
Sow	To scatter the seed over the ground you have prepared for planting.
Stake	To tie your plant to a sturdy stick for support. Put the stick in the ground close to the plant and gently tie the plant to the stake, taking care not to have the string dig into the plant stem. Your plant will then grow upright. You do this with bean, tomato, some vine plants, and tall varieties of some flowers.
Thin out	As your plants grow, you must take some of them out of the ground to leave room for the others to have enough air and space to grow.
Transplant	To move young plants from one place to another. You transplant when you take a plant from a pot and put it into your garden.

PART
1
OUTDOOR
GARDENING

CHAPTER 1

WHAT YOU NEED TO KNOW TO MAKE YOUR GARDEN GROW

A LIST
OF
GARDENING TOOLS

GARDENING TOOLS AND EQUIPMENT

Here is a list of gardening tools most often used:

cultivator:
for loosening the earth around roots of plants.

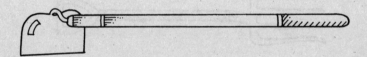

hoe:
for breaking up clumps of earth and for weeding.

hand fork:
for weeding and breaking up small areas of soil.

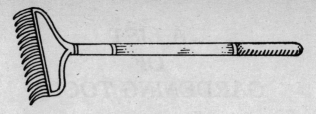

rake:
for clearing the land of debris and evening out the soil.

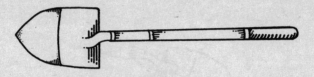

shovel:
for digging up the earth.

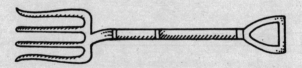

spading fork:
for digging the earth and breaking up clumps.

trowel:
for digging small holes, especially for planting.

weeder:
for removing weeds by the roots.

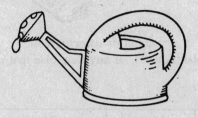

watering can:
for sprinkling your garden.

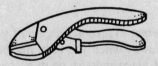

pruning shears:
for cutting away dead leaves and branches.

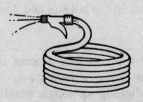

hose:
for watering your garden.

19

wagon or wheelbarrow:
for carrying plants, tools, or anything else that is heavy or large.

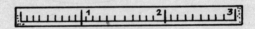

yardstick:
for measuring a garden plot.

It is very important to take good care of your gardening tools. Always put them away when you have finished using them. Keep them in a special place indoors or in a covered box. You may hang them on hooks or nails. Always clean them and dry them before you put them away. When you put your tools away for the winter, clean them and rub some oil on them so that they don't rust. Don't leave them in a damp place. If your tools do get rusty remove the rust spots with steel wool.

Don't leave your hose in the hot sun and don't run over it with the wheelbarrow.

Good digging tools you can find around the house. You can probably invent some of your own.
Apple corer—for digging up tough weeds.
Shoehorn—for digging planting holes.
Old spoon—for digging small holes.
Old fork—for cultivating.

Jonathan: *Why did Santa Claus plant a garden?*
Paul: *I don't know. Why did he?*
Jonathan: *So he could hoe! hoe! hoe!*

PREPARING A COMPOST HEAP

When you make a compost heap you are making your own fertilizer. So you will not only be growing your own garden, but also you will be feeding it. You will need help with this project, so discuss it first with a grown-up.

First you find an undisturbed place at the corner of the garden. A plot about three feet in diameter will probably be big enough. The compost heap should be contained by wire mesh. You can get wire mesh at the nursery or hardware store. Circle the area as if you were going to make a cage. The mesh should be between two and three feet high. Wire mesh allows air to circulate around the pile of food scraps and prevents odors. It will also keep out most small rodents and animals.

Listed on the next page are the kinds of foods that should be thrown on the compost heap. All the little bits of food in the compost heap eventually decay, and all the nutrients in the pile combine. Each night you throw the day's food scraps on the pile. You must *never, never* throw in any meat scraps or fat. They are not good for plants. It takes several months for the scraps of food to decompose enough for use. So your compost heap should be planned way in advance.

As the pile rots and decays, it grows smaller and smaller. When the compost heap is ready for use it will look sort of like dark brown earth that has shredded leaves mixed into it. It is very

21

light weight and has no odor. The heap should be kept moist and should be turned occasionally.

Prepare your garden plot according to instructions on page 23. Shovel the compost onto your garden plot and mix it all in very well with the earth. Then your garden is ready for planting.

Food scraps for composting:
carrot scrappings
coffee grounds and tea leaves
leftover vegetables like cabbage, broccoli, etc.
eggs and egg shells
potato skins
grass clippings
shredded newspapers
leaves, pine needles

PREPARING
A
GARDEN PLOT

You will need:

spade
gardening rake or fork
hose or watering can
fertilizer

1. Choose your site. Pick a flat area that gets lots of sun.
2. Before you begin working the ground decide on the size of your plot. Use your yardstick. A good size is 4 feet by 6 feet—just right for the beginning gardener. You will be able to grow and care for three or four different kinds of vegetables.
3. Pull up all the weeds and grasses by the roots. If the tops break off, dig up the roots of the weeds or they will begin to grow back. Clear away all the pebbles and rocks.
4. Next, turning the soil. This is kind of hard work but it is very important, so do a good job. When you see your vegetables growing you will be very proud of your labor. To turn the soil:
   a. Start at one end of your garden plot.
   b. Push the spade or fork straight down into the soil about 6 or 8 inches deep.
   c. Wiggle the spade or fork back and forth a little and lift out the clump of soil. Turn it over and put it in front of the hole.
   d. Break up the clump of earth with the edge of the spade.
   e. Only dig a small amount of earth at a time. It will be easier to lift and you can break up the lumps faster. Try to keep the ground even—no hills or lumps or deep holes.

23

   f. Keep doing this until your whole plot has been dug up and the earth broken up.

5. Rake over the ground to smooth out large lumps of earth and spread the soil evenly.

6. Now is the time to use fertilizer. If you have a compost heap (instructions on page 21) this is when you spread the compost in your garden plot. Dig it in and mix it well with the dirt. If you are not using compost, go to your local seed store or nursery and buy a bag of commercial fertilizer. Buy natural, organic fertilizer and not the chemical kind. Follow the directions on the package for the amount needed in your size garden.

7. Sprinkle the fertilizer all over the garden plot, a small area at a time. Mix it well into the earth with a spade or shovel about 6 inches deep.

8. Wet down the soil with your watering can or the gentle spray end of the hose.

9. Let the sun dry the earth before planting. Never plant in wet dirt. The seeds will rot. Don't plant when the ground is very hard and dry, either. It is too difficult.

MARKING OFF
YOUR
GARDEN PLOT

You will need:

> Four 1-foot-high stakes
> for marking off your
> garden plot
> A ball of string
> Little sticks to mark your
> planted rows
> Yardstick or tape measure

1. Using your yardstick or measuring tape, measure a 4 feet by 6 feet rectangle (or you may decide on a larger plot). Push the stakes in at each corner of the plot.
2. Tie the string to each stake and wind it all the way around the outside edge of the plot.
3. Make sure the edges of your plot are cleared of weeds so that they don't grow back over your plot. This will also clear away the places where garden pests can live.
4. Make a plan of what you want to grow. This plan will also help you keep track of what you planted until your garden starts to grow and you can see the plants. If you plant a 4- by 6-foot plot, you should have room for four or five rows of vegetables. In a 10- by 15-foot plot you will have room for about eight rows of vegetables or flowers. Some vegetables need more room to grow than others.
5. Chapter 2 lists vegetables that require a small amount of space, those that need lots of room, and those that need to be staked as they grow.

6. Using small sticks and string, mark off four or five rows as explained in step 7, spaced as suggested on the seed packet, or use the planting chart on page 41.

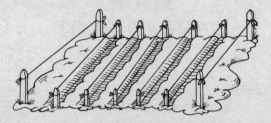

7. Pound a small stick into the earth at one end of the row. Tie the string to this stick and stretch the string straight across the plot to the spot where you want the row to end. Make sure the string is straight. Pound in the other stick in this spot and tie the string to the stick.

8. With a hand shovel dig a shallow trench about 3 inches deep under the string along the row marked. Remove the string. Plant the seeds in this trench at the right depth for whatever you are planting.

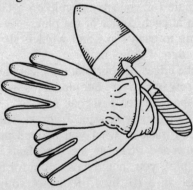

Some plants can lay down very long root systems. A single rye plant has been known to grow 378 miles of roots in only four months. Aren't you glad you didn't have to pull up that plant?

SOWING
SEEDS

When the ground is smooth and raked and all prepared, it's time to sow seeds.

The depth at which you plant seeds is very important, so follow directions carefully. Some seeds need more covering of dirt than others. The larger the seed the more earth it will need over it.

Fine seeds are usually sprinkled all the way along the row in one continuous sprinkle.

Larger seeds (like squash or pumpkin) are placed six or eight at a time in each hill.

Some seeds can begin growing when the ground is still a bit cool, early in spring. Others need warmth and sun to start life and must be planted in late spring and early summer. Read the directions to find out which is which.

If you haven't mastered the technique of sowing fine seeds, put a few scoops of earth into a bucket. Add the amount of seed you have planned to use and mix it all together well. Sprinkle the dirt and seed mixture along the row you have prepared for planting.

WHEN
YOUR PLANTS
BEGIN TO SPROUT

1. After your plants begin to sprout you should cultivate (turn) the earth around each plant very, very gently so that the earth doesn't get hard and packed down. Use the hand fork (see Vocabulary).

2. Watch for weeds even a few days after you have planted. Weeds seem to grow faster than other plants. One thing you must do is get the weeds out by their roots. Also weed around the edges of your plot so that they don't grow back. You must always be on guard for new weeds. Pull out weeds anytime you see them. As you weed, also remove dead leaves and blooms from your plants.

3. When plants are 3 to 4 inches high (or according to whenever it says on the seed package) it is time to thin them. This means pulling out some plants to allow the other plants enough space and air to grow straight and healthy. Try to pick out all plants that are weak or wilted looking. You sometimes must pull out healthy-looking plants so that you leave enough room between other plants. This is hard to do because you will care about all of your plants, but it is necessary. All plants need air and space and water. If plants are crowded together none of them will grow properly.

How plants grow. When you plant a seed under proper conditions (good soil, enough water, etc.) the seed begins to germinate and grow roots. The roots anchor the plant in the ground. Without roots plants would starve, because the roots absorb water and food and transport them to the stem.

The stem supports the leaves of the plant allowing them to get sunlight and air. It sometimes stores food, as in the cactus plant, and it brings water to the leaves.

Flowers are male and female. The female part of a flower is called the pistil, and the male part is the stamen.

As bees fly from flower to flower they carry the pollen from the stamen to the pistil of a flower which fertilizes it and causes new plants to grow.

WATERING
YOUR
GARDEN

1. When soil is dry on top, it is time to water. Give the ground a good soaking with the hose so that the water goes deep to the roots.
2. Turn the hose nozzle so the water comes out as a gentle spray. Do not use strong force which might wash away your plants.
3. Water in the morning or in the evening on sunny days. Plants don't like to be watered in the hot sun.
4. If the ground is sandy, water daily but not for too long a time.
5. If it rains, wait until the weather has been dry for two days before watering again.

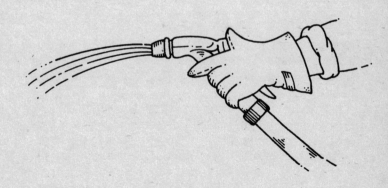

Chapter 2
Growing Your Own Vegetables

VEGETABLE GARDENING

The previous chapter has told you how to plan your garden and prepare it for your plants and seeds. Now you are ready to start your vegetable garden. There is information on the back of your seed package that will tell you the best time to plant each vegetable in your area. Your local nursery will also be able to help you, and they can tell you if you have to add any nutrients to the soil to help your garden grow. Look around your neighborhood and if there is anyone there with an especially productive garden, go and speak to him about his gardening methods. Most gardeners are eager to talk about their plants and will be pleased by your interest.

How much you plant depends on the size of your plot. If you have a small plot (4 feet by 6 feet) then you may be able to plant only three or four rows of vegetables. For a plot 6 feet by 8 feet you can generally accommodate six or seven rows of vegetables. Do not crowd your plants. It is better to grow less than to try and grow lots of things that will need more space and air than is available. It is usually a good idea to plan your garden, and then cut your plans in half. You will get much more satisfaction out of two or three rows of good healthy growing vegetables. It is very disappointing to try to grow too much and then to find that you will have to weed out most of your plants. Remember summer is fun time and you will also want to play and swim and run around. So plan a garden that will take only an hour or so out of your day to care for.

What you plant and how much to plant depends on how much space you have.

In this chapter we will tell you how to plant some vegetables that will be most satisfying. They are easy to grow, healthy for you, and fun to eat.

Look at the Planting Chart on page 41 and figure out how many rows of different kinds of vegetables you can plant. Use your yardstick or measuring tape and see how much room each vegetable needs to grow properly.

WHEN TO PLANT

There are some vegetables that can be planted in spring and others that must be planted in early summer. Under each vegetable listed we have suggested the time for planting. Seed packets also will tell you when to plant according to where you live.

1. Draw up your garden plan, marking each row with the name of the vegetable you're going to plant and when you planted it.
2. A reasonable plan for a small garden (4 by 6 feet) would be a row of carrots, a row of beets, a row of radishes and a row of lettuce.

3. Mark off rows the proper distance apart, using small stakes or sticks and long pieces of string. For each row use two sticks and a piece of string the length of the row you plan:
   a. Hammer a stake in at one end of the row.
   b. Tie the string to the stake and stretch the string straight across the plot to where you want the row to end. Make the row as straight as possible. Pound in a stake at the other end of the row and tie a string to it.
   c. In the straight line under the string, and using the string as a guide, dig a very shallow trench about 3 inches deep with a hand shovel.
4. The seeds will be planted in this trench according to directions for spacing and depth. Look at the Planting Chart on page 41. When the seeds are sown in the trench, push the dirt over the seeds from both sides. Cover them with about ½ inch of dirt, unless the directions call for deeper planting. Pat the earth down firmly over your seeds.

   When you have planted the seeds in a row remove the string and attach the seed packet or a piece of cardboard with the name of the vegetable to one of the stakes. This will mark where you have planted each vegetable.
5. Always buy good seeds. Each package of seeds should have a date stamped on it. Make sure the date on the package is the same as the year you are planting.
6. When your seeds have been planted and covered over with dirt, wet the area down gently with your watering can. Be sure to do this very carefully because you don't want to wash your seeds away.

Jonathan: *I just bought a farm. It's two miles long and one inch wide.*

Paul: *What can you plant on a farm two miles long and an inch wide?*

Jonathan: *Spaghetti!*

EASY GROWERS
FOR YOUR
FIRST SPRING CROP

You can have Bibb lettuce, scallions, and radishes. If you start in the fall you can have the first homegrown salad on your block. Choose the area you are going to use for your garden in the fall. Dig up the ground by using your shovel and rake, and churn up the earth. Leave the ground rough. When you dig up the earth, pile the soil up so that this plot is a little higher than the surrounding area and it will drain and thaw out more quickly in the spring. This area will be ready much sooner than the rest of the garden.

Radishes: Radishes are beautiful to grow; they come up very quickly and you can sometimes get in three or four crops before the season ends. There are red and white radishes.

1. Plant radishes early in the spring after you have prepared your garden.

2. Sow seeds ½ inch deep in rows 10 to 12 inches apart. When the leaves begin to sprout, thin out your plants so that they are 2 inches apart.

3. Radishes grow underground and what you see above ground are the leaves. When radishes are ready to be picked—about three weeks after planting—wash them well, put a little salt on them, and are they delicious!

Lettuce: There are many types of lettuce to choose from. Tom Thumb lettuce is a tiny head of lettuce—kid size, and fun to grow. You can start Bibb lettuce early in the season because it doesn't like the hot summer sun. You might like to start with that. Then you can grow Simpson, cos, or iceberg, which grows best in full sun with plenty of watering.

1. Plant three or four heads at a time leaving two weeks between planting. No matter how delicious lettuce is, it is hard to eat twenty heads of lettuce in one week. You can re-fertilize the land as you pick the lettuce, and plant more heads. In that way you will have two or three crops before the season ends.

2. Check your package, or if you are using plants you bought at a nursery, ask the person there how far apart they should be planted.
3. The rows should be 18 to 20 inches apart and the seeds sown ½ inch deep. When plants are 2 inches high, thin them out 6 to 12 inches apart, depending on the type of lettuce you plant.
4. Feed your lettuce plants with a water-soluble plant food if you wish.

Scallions: You can get little onion plants at the nursery or you can plant seeds.
1. Sow the seeds ½ inch deep in rows 12 inches apart early in the spring.
2. If the soil is poor, put in peat moss and work it into the soil before planting seeds. You will see little sprouts in about 12 days.
3. When your plants are 3 inches high, thin them out so that your plants are 3 inches apart.
4. Dig around the plants with the garden hoe or small shovel as they are growing. This helps air move around the soil and helps the plants grow.
5. Pull out weeds frequently.
6. When the tops of the onions droop over, the plants are ready to harvest. Pull out the onions and let them dry on the ground. Do not leave them in the ground after the tops droop.

Carrots:

1. Make rows 12 to 15 inches apart.
2. Sow seeds ¼ inch deep in fine soil, pressed down gently.
3. Carrots are slow to germinate. In dry weather, you should gently water the seed bed daily for two weeks after planting to ensure better germination.
4. When the plants are 2 inches high, thin them out to 2 inches apart. This is very important. Carrots will not grow well if they don't have plenty of room.
5. Be very sure that you always weed carefully.
6. You can harvest your crop when the carrot root is ½ to ¾ inch in diameter at the top.
7. Carrots can be planted all during the spring and early summer.

Jonathan:	*Are carrots really good for the eyesight?*
Paul:	*Well, have you ever seen a rabbit wearing glasses?*

PLANTING CHART

VEGETABLE	DEPTH TO PLANT (in inches)	SPACE BETWEEN PLANTS (in inches)	SPACE BETWEEN ROWS (in inches)
Beans	2	6	18
Beets	1	3	12
Carrots	½	3	12
Lettuce	½	3	12
Radishes	½	1	12
Tomatoes	½	24 to 36	36
Corn	2	18	24
Cucumbers	½	36 to 48	36
Onions	¼	4	12
Scallions	½	1½	12
Summer Squash	1	24	36 to 48
Pumpkins	1	48 to 72	48 to 72

41

OTHER
GARDEN
VEGETABLES

Peas: These are cool weather plants. They cannot germinate in hot weather. They can be planted in late March or early April, if the soil is workable.

Plant dwarf varieties. These are easier to grow because you don't have to stake them, and they take up little room. Try snow peas because you can eat them pod and all. Yummy!

1. Cultivate the soil and plant your seeds 1 inch deep.
2. The distance between rows should be 28 inches.
3. Pack soil down over seeds gently.
4. Seeds will germinate in 7 to 10 days.
5. Gently water seedlings often. Water in the afternoon so the leaves will have a chance to dry off before nightfall. Too much water may cause disease organisms to form on the leaves.
6. Thin out your plants so that there is no pushing and shoving for air and space.
7. Place a little fertilizer beside each plant when it is 2 inches high.
8. Some pea plants may need staking as they grow so that they won't fall over.

Beans: If you want to plant string beans (or snap beans as they are sometimes called) or just beans, it's better to plant the kind called bush beans because you don't have to use long stakes to hold them up, as you do with regular pole beans. That's a lot of extra trouble. Plant bush beans in the spring when it's really warm in your area—anytime after May 1.

1. Measure off a row 2 feet from the next row on each side.
2. Dig holes 1½ inches deep and 4 inches apart from the next hole.
3. Place three or four seeds in each hole.
4. Cover over with dirt in a little mound and pat down firmly.
5. When your plants start to grow and are about 3 inches high, thin them out to six to ten plants to each foot (use your yardstick).
6. Don't work on your bean plants while the vines are wet.
7. Pick beans while they are young and tender. A bean should break off the vine with a snap—that's why they're called snap beans. Harvest your beans frequently. The more you pick, the more will grow.

Mustard Greens: This vegetable is very tasty and tangy. You can cook them or eat them raw in salad. And like most green, leafy vegetables, they're very good for you.

1. Start planting as early in the spring as you like—just as soon as you can dig up the soil without a struggle.
2. Make your rows 12 inches apart.
3. Sow the seeds along the row ¼ inch deep. Cover with soil and pat it down firmly.
4. When the plants are 2 inches high, thin them out to 5 inches apart.
5. After they've grown, keep picking them, just enough for each meal. They keep growing all summer. One row 7 feet long will be enough for your family all summer.

Beets:

1. Can be sown early in spring.

2. Cultivate the soil deeply.

3. Seeds should be planted 1 inch deep. Pat soil over them gently.

4. The rows should be 18 inches apart.

5. Seeds should germinate in 14 to 18 days.

6. When plants are 1 inch high, begin to thin them out. As they get taller, thin them out so that they are 6 inches apart.

7. Beets will come to full maturity in approximately 55 days.

8. Beets should be harvested when small, young, and tender.

Tomatoes: Once healthy tomato plants get started, there's no stopping them. A few plants can provide tomatoes for your whole family. Start your tomatoes with small plants from the nursery instead of seeds because they grow slowly. Four or five plants is all you will need. Find out from the nursery which tomato plants do best in your area. Be sure that the plants you buy look very sturdy and are green in color.

1. Be sure to choose a very sunny spot in your garden because tomatoes do best in full sunshine. Plan to plant your tomatoes when winter is definitely over and the weather warms up to at least 60 degrees each day for a week.
2. Prepare the ground, making sure you remove all weeds and rocks. Turn the soil and chop it up so it is free of lumps.
3. The soil should be moist but not too wet. Plant your tomatoes as soon as possible after you get your plants home from the nursery.
4. Dig a hole 2 or 3 inches deeper than the earth the plant was growing in in the plant box. This should make your hole 5 or 6 inches deep. Space the holes 2½ feet apart.
5. Put each plant in its hole carefully and firm the earth down around each plant. Leave a slight depression around the plant so that water will be retained close to the plant.
6. After all your tomato plants are in the ground, give each plant a cupful of water-soluble fertilizer (follow directions on the package). This will give your plants an extra boost toward healthy growth.
7. Two weeks after planting, give your tomatoes another cupful of fertilizer.
8. Cultivate the earth around your plants. Pull all the weeds out from around your plants very frequently.
9. When your plants are 1 foot high you should stake them. Staking prevents your plants from falling over onto the ground, where there is more chance they will rot.
10. Follow our instructions for staking your plants on page 12.
11. Pinch off the small shoots on the main stem so that all the nourishment goes into the main stem. These small shoots are near the leaves and should be pinched off very carefully so that the main stem is not injured. You may also pinch off the top of your plant as it grows. (See Vocabulary.)
12. Pick your tomatoes when they are red and ripe. If there is a sudden frost before your tomatoes are ripe, cover your plants with burlap or polyethylene or old lightweight blankets. You may be able to save them and have more weeks of nice tomatoes ripening on the vine. Or pick the green

tomatoes and wrap two or three at a time in heavy layers of newspaper and store them in a dark, cool place where they will ripen slowly.

Paul:	*How much are those tomatoes?*
Grocer:	*Twenty-five cents a pound.*
Paul:	*Oh! Did you raise them yourself?*
Grocer:	*Yep. Yesterday they were twenty cents a pound.*

VEGETABLES
THAT
TAKE UP SPACE

These are vegetables that take up lots of room, so decide beforehand very carefully just what you want to plant, and allow enough space. It is perfectly all right to plant one or two different types of vegetables instead of a whole lot. For instance you may just want to grow pumpkins for Halloween.

Pumpkins: Plant after all danger of frost has passed.
1. Cultivate your soil and make sure all the weeds are pulled out.
2. Pumpkins grow on small hills. So, scoop out one or two shovelfuls of soil.
3. Put in a handful of fertilizer and work well into the soil.

46

4. Replace the soil you shoveled out and mound it up into a little hill about 3 inches above the ground and about 18 inches around.
5. Plant five or six seeds 1 inch deep in each hill.
6. Press soil down well.
7. Hills should be 4 to 6 feet apart from each other (see, we told you that lots of room was needed). Water after seeding, very gently.
8. Pumpkins should sprout in about 7 to 10 days.
9. When plants are 6 inches tall, thin out each hill to three of the hardiest looking plants.
10. Keep your pumpkin patch free of weeds.
11. When you cultivate your soil as the plants are growing, use a hand weeder so that your plants won't be injured.
12. By Halloween you should be able to carve a pretty scary face into a pumpkin you have grown yourself.

Cucumbers: Cucumbers like to spread out a lot too. Not only that, once cucumbers start growing they sort of burst out in enthusiasm, and from a few plants you will usually get more cucumbers than you know what to do with. So, plant just a few hills (one or two) and you'll still probably have enough to share with friends and neighbors. There are two kinds of cucumbers:

One for slicing in salad, and the other kind is for pickling. Make sure you read the label on the seed packet to see that you have the kind you want.

1. Plant seeds in the late spring or early summer.
2. Make two or three hills (as described in directions for pumpkins). Dig them 4 or 5 feet apart. Work in a little fertilizer before sowing seeds.
3. Put eight seeds in each hill and cover ½ inch deep.
4. When the plants have grown 4 inches tall, thin to three or four in each hill. Cultivate (with a hand cultivator) frequently, so that the earth doesn't get packed in.
5. Once your cucumbers begin to turn green, turn them over so that the sun will ripen them on all sides.
6. Don't let the cucumbers grow very large because they will be tough and full of seeds.

Summer Squash: There are many different kinds of squash divided into two categories—winter squash and summer squash. Summer squash comes in different sizes, shapes, and colors. But it's all called summer squash and the directions for planting are the same for whichever kind you like—Patty Pan squash, yellow summer squash, or green zucchini.

1. Sow seeds in late spring or early summer.
2. Dig hills 2 feet apart and make rows 4 feet apart.
3. Plant eight seeds 1 inch deep in each hill.

4. When plants are 2 to 3 inches tall, thin out to the three strongest plants in each hill.

5. Cultivate around each plant to loosen the soil a bit.

Always water gently but thoroughly after you plant any seeds. This helps them to get started growing.

HARVESTING YOUR CROP

Pick vegetables when they are just ripe, or slightly under-ripe for tomatoes—let them ripen on a sunny windowsill—so that you eat them at the peak of flavor.

Pick lettuce and leafy vegetables, corn, peas, and beans just before you intend to eat them. Make sure your garden plot is never too dry. Water well the day before you plan to pick your vegetables to ensure extra moisture and fresh flavor.

One or two rows of soybeans or "stinky" marigolds planted all around your garden will keep away pesky garden animals. They don't like them.

Those pesky creatures also don't like noise. If you have a spare portable radio and don't mind leaving it out in the garden at night it helps keep away the thieving rabbits, woodchucks, etc.

CHAPTER
3
HOW TO
GROW FLOWERS
FROM SEEDS

GROWING
A FLOWER GARDEN
FROM SEED

When starting a flower garden, it is a good idea to start with annuals. (See Vocabulary.) You can plant hardy annuals as soon as the ground can be worked. Half-hardy annuals should be sown after all danger of frost has passed.

PREPARING
A FLOWER
GARDEN PLOT

Choose a sunny location on level ground with good drainage not
too near shrubs and trees. Follow our instructions for preparing
your garden plot given in Chapter 1. Make your garden plan. A
good-sized plot for the beginning gardener is about 4 by 6 feet
or 6 by 8 feet. Select flowers that you can grow by seed suc-
cessfully in your area. Choose tall, medium, and short plants.
Tall plants are planted in the back of your garden plot, then
medium sized plants, and then, in the front, your smaller flowers.
If your garden is in the middle of your yard rather than against
a wall or fence, plant the tall flowers in the center of your garden
plot, with the medium height flowers around them and the short
flowers around the edge.

Plant your seeds in straight rows. Choose plants which don't
require special soil or more sun than your plot has. If you choose
plants for color as well as size, your garden will be prettier and
more interesting to look at. If you have room, for instance, ele-
phants ears (caladium) are fun to grow. They grow 6 feet tall
and have great big leaves which look friendly and floppy. Plant
them late in May in well-spaded soil. They are easy to grow but
need lots of water. Or try growing nasturiums, which not only
have pretty flowers, but also very tasty leaves you can serve in
salad.

You can select the flowers you want to plant by sending away
for seeds from the seed catalogues. If you order from catalogues,
be sure that you do it early enough to allow time for the seeds
to reach you before planting time. Or you can visit your local
seed or gardening store and examine the seed packets there. That

would also be a good time to have a conversation with the store owner about what plants grow well in your area.

Prepare your garden plot by clearing the ground and cultivating it. The soil should be slightly moist and crumbly in texture. Mark off your rows with stakes and strings and make shallow trenches about ½ inch deep.

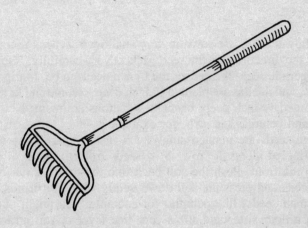

SOWING
YOUR
SEEDS

Most flower seeds are sown in very shallow trenches. You must follow the directions on the seed packets very carefully. Usually, the larger the seed, the deeper the trench needs to be. Marigolds, zinnias, and dahlias are planted ½ inch deep; cleome and larkspur are planted ⅜ inch deep; bachelor's buttons are planted ¼ inch deep; and petunias ¹⁄₁₆ inch, for example.

Large seeds are planted singly, 1½ inches apart. Tiny seeds are sprinkled along the row. Sow seeds from the back of your plot to the front. Push the soil back into the trenches on top of your seeds and press the soil down gently with your hands. For very small seeds, like petunia, for example, you might put the soil in a flour sifter and sift a very fine layer of soil on top of your seeds. Press down very gently. After sowing, water your garden with a gentle, fine spray. Soil must be kept moist while seeds germinate. If they get dry they may not germinate and grow roots at all. However, don't overwater because the seeds may rot or be washed away.

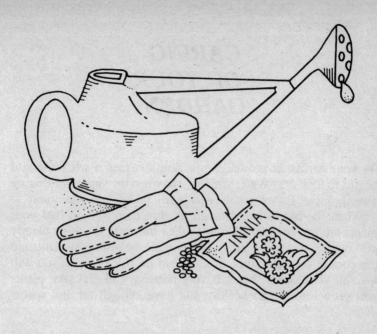

The largest seed in the world is the double coconut which grows in the Seychelles. It weighs 40 pounds. How would you like to have to plant that?

CARING
FOR YOUR
GARDEN

As your garden is growing, you should water it when the soil begins to look dry. Water your garden when the sun is not shining directly on it. Either water in the early or the late afternoon.

When the plants begin to grow, thin them out so that your plants are not crowded. Do this when the earth is moist. Gently pull out the weakest looking plants until the strongest plants are the correct distance apart. It's hard to do this because you will love all your plants, but it is very necessary so that your plants will grow strong and healthy and have enough air and space.

Cultivate and weed your garden with a hand tool once a week. Taller plants such as giant zinnias, marigolds, and cosmos may need staking.

Cut off the faded flowers as soon as they begin to die and the plants will bloom for a longer period of time.

If you plant certain flowers in your garden you can attract rare and beautiful birds such as the hummingbird and the goldfinch. They like columbine, petunia, phlox, and Vesper iris. The goldfinch likes the seeds of the sunflower, goldenrod, and thistle. Hummingbirds and butterflies are also attracted by the blooms of the butterfly bush.

PICKING YOUR FLOWERS

You will have enough flowers to pick some for your house and still leave plenty of plants in your garden, so that it looks beautiful.

Pick flowers early in the morning before the heat of the day or in the evening after the sun has gone down because they will last longer. Don't worry, others will grow.

Put cut flowers into lukewarm water immediately after picking. Add 1 teaspoon of plant food to water. When you cut flowers, cut the stems at a slant and not straight across. They will absorb more water that way.

Pull off the leaves and blooms on the lower stems of the flowers.

Always put cut flowers into a clean container and don't crowd them.

How would you like to pick a flower weighing 15 pounds and measuring 3 feet across? All you have to do is go to Southeast Asia and pluck a *Rafflesia arnoldi*, which is a lily plant growing there. What a bouquet several of those would make!

A LIST OF ANNUALS, BIENNIALS, AND PERENNIALS

EASY ANNUALS

zinnia
marigold
pink
celosia (Forest fire)
petunia
sweet alyssum
four-o'clock
bachelor's button
ageratum
aster
cleome
phlox
portulaca

EASY BIENNIALS

chinese lantern
foxglove
forget-me-not
hollyhock
pansy
baby's breath

EASY PERENNIALS AND BIENNIALS TO PLANT FROM SEEDS

chrysanthemum
hibiscus
rudbeckia
salvia
English daisy
Canterbury bell
delphinium
sunflower
candytuft
sweet pea
common sedum
common sweet white viola
Shasta daisy
lily of the valley
bleeding heart
bluebell

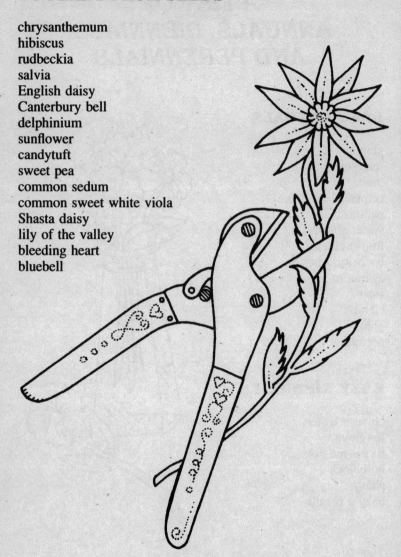

Paul:	*What kind of flowers are you growing? Roses?*
Jonathan:	*No. Chrysanthemums.*
Paul:	*They look like roses.*
Jonathan:	*Well they are chrysanthemums.*
Paul:	*How do you spell it?*
Jonathan:	*K-r-e-s-, no—umm, krys—er. Come to think of it, maybe they are roses.*

CHAPTER 4

PLANT A SPRING BULB GARDEN

SPRING
BULB
GARDEN

A spring bulb garden should be planted in the fall. Select a site with good drainage so that ice cannot collect around the bulbs. Plant the bulbs in little groups so they will look natural in a space that gets lots of sun.

1. Always plant bulbs pointed side up—flat side down.
2. Once you plant bulbs, they will come up every year. Not only that, they will multiply, so eventually you can separate them in the fall and plant more bulbs in new places.

Here are some kinds of bulbs that will give you a very jolly flower garden in the spring, before your flowers planted from seeds begin to grow.

CROCUS

This is an inexpensive bulb for you to buy. Crocuses come in many different colors. You can plant them at the end of September. The first crocuses poking up through the wintery ground tell you that spring is on the way. Sometimes they even come up through the snow. Crocuses can be planted practically anywhere. They look nice as a border along the lawn or planted among shrubs or in any patch of earth that will catch the sun's rays. Plant the bulbs 3 to 4 inches deep, 2 to 3 inches apart. Always put them in the ground with the pointy end upwards.

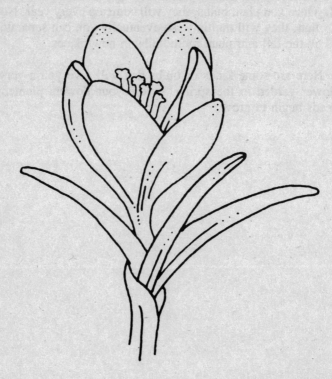

TULIP

Pretty, cheery flowers that bloom from early spring to late in May.

Plant tulip bulbs in a sunny location with good drainage from the end of October until the ground freezes. They should be planted from 4 to 6 inches apart, 6 to 8 inches deep.

DAFFODIL
AND
NARCISSUS

Daffodils and narcissi are in the same family.

Plant new bulbs in the early autumn. Small bulbs should be planted about 3 inches deep and 3 or 4 inches apart. Large varieties should be planted 6 inches deep and 6 inches apart. The base of the bulb should rest on very firm earth (no air pockets underneath). Plant a few and you'll soon have a lot. Separate them when they multiply—they won't bloom well when there are too many.

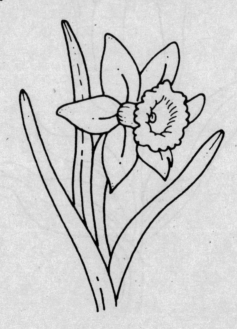

IRIS

There are many types of iris. They are called bearded or plain. Some are tall, some short or dwarf, in a variety of colors. They make a lovely border and are also good in rock gardens. Good drainage and sun are very important wherever you plant them.

Plant tall iris 15 to 18 inches apart and 2 inches deep.

Plant dwarf varieties 5 to 6 inches apart and 2 inches deep.

These bulbs should not be planted deeply, and the soil should be firmly packed around them.

SNOWDROP

Pretty, little flowers which actually grow under the snow tell you spring is coming even before the crocus lets you know.

Plant them in a damp place, mostly in shade, not full sun. If you want to divide and transplant them, do it while they are growing, not resting. Plant them 3 to 4 inches apart, about 2 or 3 inches deep.

CHAPTER 5

MAKE A ROCK GARDEN

1. Choose a sunny or partially shaded slope or hill with good drainage for your rock garden.
2. Clear the land of weeds and stones, but save the large rocks.
3. Buy good, rich topsoil for your rockery, and work it into the soil.
4. Place rocks in a pleasing design and leave lots of space between rocks for your plants.
5. Try to make the arrangement look as natural as possible. Don't place rocks in a straight row.
6. You can put shade plants in the sun but sun-loving plants can't be planted in the shade.

   Some plants good for a rock garden are:

alyssum	hens and chicks
candytuft	Viola Jersey Gem-Violet
columbine	forget-me-not
catnip	wood cress
pinks	bellflowers
wood sorrel	thyme
sedum	phlox
myrtle	

7. Check your nursery for the best plants to grow in your area.

CHAPTER
6

OUTDOOR
PLANTING
UNDER GLASS

Sometime around March or early April, when the weather begins to look good, you may get the urge to do some outdoor planting. But since it may still be too cool to ensure plant growth, try this in a sunny corner of your garden.

You will need:

large-necked jars
    without lids
flower seeds or
    small plants
fertilizer

1. Churn up the earth and remove all rocks, stones, or weeds.
2. Mix in a little fertilizer.
3. Plant seeds in small area about the size of the neck of your bottle or jar. If you have four jars you can space your seeds about 10 to 12 inches apart. Sprinkle several seeds in each area and cover with soil.
4. Water.
5. Place the jar, upside-down, on the seeded area.
6. The glass will protect your seeds from the cool weather, but will let the sun shine on them so that they will be warm and nourished.

7. Pick up your jar every few days or so, and if the earth around your plant is dry, use your watering can to sprinkle the area around your plant. Cover the seeded area with the jar again.

8. When your plant has grown about 6 inches and the weather is warmer, remove the jar and your plant will have had a head start toward its spring blooming.

PART 2
GARDENING INDOORS

CHAPTER
7
INTERESTING
INDOOR PLANTS

PLANTING
BULBS

Wouldn't it be lovely to have flowers blooming in your house during the cold weather! While you are putting on your boots and woolen mittens you can see a tulip or a daffodil or a hyacinth nodding to you on your window ledge; a reminder that the snow will soon melt and you had better begin thinking about some spring planting. You can have bulbs flowering in your home from October to early spring.

To grow bulbs in the winter, you have to fool the bulbs into thinking it's spring. So put them into the back of the refrigerator in a paper bag for 2-3 weeks. They'll think it's winter. Then take them out and plant them according to directions. They'll bloom because they'll think it's spring. Here are some of the varieties to use:

NARCISSUS

You will need:

      three to six narcissus bulbs
      wide, shallow bowl twice
        the depth of the bulbs
      pebbles, gravel or pearl
        chips

You can plant in early October:
1. Fill the bowl about two-thirds full of pebbles or gravel or chips.
2. Place the bulbs in the bowl root side down. Place close together.

3. Add water just to cover pebbles.
4. Fill with the rest of pebbles until only the top of the bulbs show.
5. Place in cool area. (Not on top of the radiator.)
6. Narcissi will flower in 3 to 5 weeks.
   Here are some varieties of tender narcissi you can use:
   paper white
   Chinese sacred lily
   grand soleil d'or

HYACINTH

You will need:
   large hyacinth bulb
   hyacinth glass or jar in which
      bulb can be suspended
   toothpicks

1. Push three toothpicks into the bulb, spaced evenly around the pit.
2. Place bulb in jar (root side down), suspended with toothpicks.
3. Fill glass with water to root end of bulb.
4. Cover bulb loosely with aluminum foil.
5. Place in the back of refrigerator or in a cool, dark closet until roots have grown. This takes a long time, about 2 months, so tell your mother not to throw out the jar.
5. After roots appear, remove from cool, dark place and put into cool, light area. A window ledge that does not get direct sunlight is suitable for about 2 weeks.
6. After this, you can place your bulbs on any table or window and enjoy the flowers.

AMARYLLIS

You can plant from December to March.

You will need:

        amaryllis bulbs
        6-inch pot
        soil or bulb mixture

1. Fill your pot half full of watered soil.
2. Place bulb in soil and cover with more soil until only the top of bulb is showing.
3. Water well after planting, but do not water again until the bulb sprouts. Then feed with liquid fertilizer.
4. Water lightly several times until flowers appear.
5. After the bulb has flowered, water frequently for about 2 weeks. Then keep dry and let leaves die.
6. Store in a dark, cool place (basement or closet) until the following January when buds will appear. At that time scrape off about 1 inch of soil and replace with fresh new soil which contains fertilizer. You can enjoy this same plant year after year if you take good care of it after flowering.

If you live in an apartment and good soil is not available, buy potting soil, or a mixture of vermiculite and perlite for your pots and window boxes and you will grow healthy plants. You can get these in the 5 and 10, hardware store, or local nursery.

CACTUS

Cactus is easy to grow. Since it is a desert plant it needs very little water—about every ten days and less in the winter when it "rests." Be sure the earth is dry before watering and water the earth only, not the plant. Be careful not to stick yourself on the sharp cactus needles.

There are many kinds of cactuses. Under the right conditions most will flower. There are some that require special care, but here's an easy one. It's a very common one so don't let the strange name throw you. It's called *echinopsis* and can be bought in any plant store. It is easy to grow. All it needs is a little good, rich soil, sunlight, and water every now and then. If it flowers, the blooms will be white or pale pink. If it doesn't, that's okay. It will still be pretty to look at.

You will need:

a rectangular fish tank. (It's pretty to look at cactus through glass.) Or any shape flowerpot will do.
rich soil

1. Place about 2 inches of soil at the bottom of your fish tank.
2. Place your cactus plants in the soil and pat the earth down around the plants.
3. You can plant different varieties of cactuses together.
4. Water very sparingly every 10 days or so with lukewarm water. Cold water will shock your cactus plants.
5. Place on window ledge but not right up against the window, because if it's cold outside your container will also get cold.

Some interesting cactuses are: stone face, rat tail cactus, base-ball plant, zebra havorthia, golden stars, old man cactus and Christmas cactus.

WINDOW-BOX
HERBS

Herbs can grow indoors all year long. They look pretty growing near a sunny kitchen window, and your mother can cut them anytime she wants to add flavor to her cooking. You can also grow herbs to give as presents. After your herbs have grown you can transplant them to a pretty clay pot which you can decorate. An interesting way to decorate your pot would be to turn a clay pot upside down on a glass jar (this makes it easier to paint and no messy fingerprints). Paint the outside of your pot (never paint the inside). When the pot is dry, turn it right side up and carefully print the name of the herb on the pot. Then transplant the herb to your decorated pot and someone will be awfully impressed with your lovely present.

Some easy-growing herbs are: chives, parsley, mint, dill, savory, thyme, and marjoram.

You will need:

packets of herb seeds or small
potted herbs from the seed
store
small clay pots
good rich soil

1. Fill your pot three-quarters full of soil.
2. Place your plant or seeds in the pot.
3. Cover with a ½ inch more soil.

4. Push the soil down gently.
5. Water your plants and put them in a sunny window.
6. Water every 4 to 5 days, sparingly.
7. When your herbs have grown to 4 or 5 inches you can begin cutting them for use. Snip off as much as you need from the top of the plant. They will grow again quickly. Keep cutting and they will keep growing. Cut off blades or leaves.
8. Water every 4 or 5 days. Keep chives well watered.

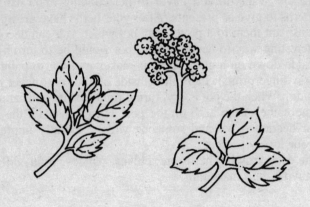

ALL KINDS
OF
PLANTERS

1. Collect planters from any place. Loaf pans, biscuit tins, aluminum pans, wooden boxes, or plastic boxes are just a few containers that can be used. Choose a planter that won't rust or rot. Ask your mom's advice.
2. You can leave the containers the natural color or you can paint or decorate them first. Be sure to wait until the paint is absolutely dry before you plant anything in them.
3. Add a few small rocks or some broken pieces from a clay flowerpot for drainage.
4. Buy some potting soil, or if you have a backyard you can get some dirt there and put that into your container. Add some plant food at this time.
5. You can now plant a little clump of chives or a cutting from a philodendron plant or an ivy plant. (See page 117.) Ask your mother if there is a special herb or flower that she likes best and then you can plant that and have a wonderful gift for her when the plant grows big enough to clip.
6. Set your container garden on a window ledge in the sun and water it gently twice a week.

You can plant plants in almost anything. Thinking up interesting planters is fun. Plant small plants in muffin tins, cut-off milk cartons, frozen juice cans, egg cartons, paper cups, or even in egg shells. You can probably think up lots of others.

When plants are growing and healthy and begin to get too large for their containers, you can transplant them to other containers you've created.

Plants in egg shells or cartons, paper cups, and other containers which disintegrate can be transplanted into your garden or window box container and all.

CHAPTER
8
PLANTS FROM YOUR KITCHEN

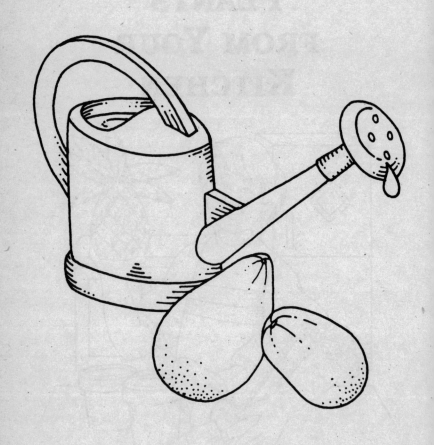

TWO WAYS
TO GROW
AN AVOCADO

You will need:

> knife
> three toothpicks
> glass of water
> 5- or 6-inch pot
> package of potting soil

1. After you eat the avocado save the pit and wash it off very thoroughly.
2. Make an X cut with a knife on the wide, flat end of your avocado pit. This will make it easier for the root to push out.
3. Push three toothpicks around the wide, flat side of the pit. Space them evenly around the pit.
4. Suspend the pit in a glass of water with the wide end about ½ inch into the water. The toothpicks will support the pit on the edge of the glass.
5. Keep adding water as it evaporates so that the water level stays the same and the bottom of the pit doesn't dry up.
6. Place the pit on a window ledge but not in direct sunlight.
7. In about 4 to 6 weeks a root will sprout.
8. When the root is 4 to 5 inches long, the pit is ready to plant in soil.
9. Fill your pot half full of soil. Remove the toothpicks from your pot. Carefully fill in the rest of your earth, patting it gently around your pit to within 1 inch of the top of the pit.
10. Put the pot in a sunny window and water your plant often. When your plant is about a foot tall, pinch off the top shoot. This will help the side branches grow and your plant will be leafy and full.

HERE IS THE SECOND WAY
TO GROW AN AVOCADO

You will need:

> glass
> 4-inch flowerpot
> rich soil
> large flowerpot for transplanting

1. After you eat the avocado save the pit and wash it off very thoroughly.
2. Soak it in a glass of water for 2 days.
3. Peel off the skin. After soaking, it should come off easily.
4. Fill the flowerpot with soil almost to the top (about ½ inch from top).
5. Make a hole for the pit and plant it flat end down. Half inch of pit should stick up out of the soil.
6. Put the pot in a window but not in direct sunlight. Water well every few days. When it starts to sprout put the plant in the sun.
7. When the plant grows well and leaves are sprouting, pinch off new leaves growing on the top so that your plant will spread out and grow fuller and higher.
8. Transplant to a larger pot when the plant is about 2 feet tall.

PLANTING TOPS
OF
VEGETABLES

You will need:

> 1-inch top of carrot, beet, parsnip,
>   or turnip
> shallow dish
> water or sand

1. Cut off about 1 inch of the top of a beet, parsnip, carrot, or turnip.
2. Fill a shallow dish with ½ inch of water or wet sand.
3. Place your top, cut side down, in the water or sand.
4. If you plant in water, be sure to add enough water to the dish as it evaporates. If you plant in sand, water about 2 times a week.

LENTILS AND
MUNG BEANS
GROW LIKE CRAZY

Lentils grow like a forest. Spread a layer of lentils in a saucer and add enough water to moisten (not too much). Put the saucer in a sunny place and in 2 or 3 days they will sprout. Follow these directions for mung beans too. Sprinkle mung beans and lentil sprouts on your salad. They are nice and crunchy.

GROW
A
PINEAPPLE PLANT

You will need:

       pineapple top
       shallow dish
       sand
       soil
       pot

1. Slice off leafy top of pineapple, leaving about 1 inch of the fruit attached.
2. Let the plant dry for a few days to avoid fungus.
3. Put some moist sand in a dish and place your pineapple, fruit side down, into 1 inch of sand.
4. Place plant on window ledge but out of direct sunlight.
5. When leaves appear, replant pineapple in pot with soil and then place on sunny window ledge.
6. Water as needed.

HOW TO GROW
A
SWEET POTATO

You will need:

  sweet potato
  toothpicks
  glass
  soil
  pot

1. Fill a crock or mug or any jar you can't see through three quarters full of water.
2. Stick four toothpicks one-third of the way up from the narrow root end of your sweet potato. The toothpicks will support your plant in the water.
3. Place the potato in a jar with the root end down.
4. Put it in a sunny window, and little shoots will start to grow.
5. Cut off all but three or four of the sturdiest shoots so that your plant will grow stronger and fuller.
6. When you have lots of roots and good sturdy shoots, transplant into soil in a pot and keep well watered in the sun.

PLANTING
A
CITRUS PLANT

You will need:

> lemon, grapefruit, or orange
>   pits
> 6-inch pot
> potting soil

Fill the pot with the potting soil. When you eat fruit, instead of throwing the seeds away, push them into the soil. Water the plant and keep it in a sunny window. The seeds will grow and who knows, someday you may even have an orange or lemon tree of your own.

Florida gardener:	*(Picking up a watermelon) Is this the biggest grapefruit you can grow?*
California gardener:	*Hey! Careful, you're crushing that raisin.*

GROWING
A
"WHATSIS" PLANT

You will need:

    large pot
    potting soil
    all kinds of seeds and pits

Fill a large pot with potting soil. Into this push the seeds of whatever fruit it is you happen to be eating. Water and keep it in a sunny window. Eventually, some will grow, but you won't know what exactly to expect so it will be your "whatsis" plant.

Plants in pots do not get all their nourishment from the soil. They get food from water and air too. That is why a plant will grow and flourish in the same pot over a long period of time.

CHAPTER
9
PLANTING IN A PICKLE JAR (A TERRARIUM)

A terrarium is a garden under glass. It doesn't need watering or very much tending, so once you've made your terrarium all you have to do is look and enjoy its beauty.

You can use many kinds of containers, as long as it is one of clear glass, has a lid of some kind, and is roomy enough to hold the soil and plants you need. Use a container with a wide enough neck to reach your hand in.

GOOD TERRARIUM PLANTERS ARE:

a large pickle jar   cookie jar
fish bowl or fish tank   apothecary jar
wineglass or brandy snifter   large mayonnaise jar
glass pitcher

PLANTS TO GROW
IN A TERRARIUM ARE:

small fern
columbine
hepatica
wintergreen
partridge berry vine
mosses
coleus
baby's tears
dwarf begonias
violas
ivy
tiny evergreens
prayer plant
selaginella
acorn

YOU WILL NEED:

small plants
glass container and lid of glass or plastic
a long stick or knitting needle to make holes in earth
pebbles or rocks for decoration
clean soil
coarse gravel
small pieces of charcoal
bleach and water to sterilize container
water and cloth to clean leaves of plants
paintbrush

1. Wash your container thoroughly. Fill it up with a solution of bleach and warm water (3 cups of water to 1 cup of bleach). Let it stand for half an hour.
2. Rinse container out *very thoroughly* and let it stand upside down to drain. Your container must be perfectly dry before you begin.
3. Put a one-inch-deep layer of coarse gravel on the bottom of the container.
4. Scatter around small pieces of charcoal to keep the earth sweet.
5. Pour in 2 inches of soil on top of gravel.
6. Moisten soil with a little bit of water, being careful not to wet the sides of the container. Don't leave any standing pools of water.
7. Before you begin, shake off any earth clinging to roots of plants and clean off the leaves.
8. With a long stick make little holes ½ inches deep in the soil to put the plants in.
9. Holding the roots of plant together, carefully press the plant in the little hole you have prepared. Press the earth down around the root. Do this with all your plants. Remember to leave room for them to grow. Brush away any dirt or leaves on sides of container with paint brush. Add interesting small rocks, pebbles or bits of mirror or colored glass, or an acorn for decoration.
10. Add a little water (¼ of a cup for 1-gallon jar) very carefully drop by drop. Use meat baster or medicine dropper.
11. Put a glass (or plastic) lid on, leaving a tiny bit of air space, or put a lid on top of pickle jar and punch air holes in it.
12. If the glass becomes cloudy remove the lid, about an hour each day, and let the terrarium air until cloudiness disappears.
13. Water a very little *only* if the earth looks dry. Terrariums get their moisture from condensation which trickles in the soil. A good terrarium can last a couple of years.
14. Put terrarium in light but not sun.

The art of growing real trees in very small sizes is called *bonsai*. These are real trees which measure as little as 8 inches high. Bonsai gardeners clip and prune the trees, which are kept in small pots so that their root systems cannot grow out very far. The plants are given a limited amount of plant food so that they can remain healthy but do not grow very much. Bonsai trees when grown and cared for properly can live hundreds of years and are very highly prized.

CHAPTER 10

How to Make a Hanging Plant and a Cutting of a Plant

MAKE
A
HANGING PLANT

A hanging plant in the window will make your room look cheerful and friendly.

If you would like to make a hanging plant get a grown-up to help you screw a hook into the window frame or ceiling. Then you will need:

A plant which grows downward and spreads in a trailing way instead of one which grows straight up in a pot. There are many kinds of such plants.

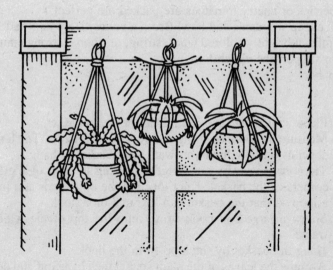

We suggest:

pothos
grape ivy
wandering
  Jerusalem

These do well in direct sun
    or bright light.

Swedish ivy
philodendron

These do well in sun but
    don't need it. Should be
    in bright light.

spider plant

Does not need direct sun,
    should have good light.

You will need:
a basket (the little plastic baskets from the supermarket in which
    berries or cherry tomatoes are packed are perfect.)
or a cheap wooden salad bowl (from a variety store or 5 and 10)
lengths of brightly colored wool, string, or ribbon (strong enough
    to support the weight)
cup hook

1. Place your plant, pot and all, in the berry basket.
2. Measure the wool or string into four equal lengths. The length
    depends on how high you want your basket to hang.
3. Tie (*very securely*) one length of string to each of the four
    corners of the basket. Knot together the other ends and make
    a loop so that the basket can be hung on a hook.
4. Screw a large cup hook firmly into the top of the window
    frame.
5. Hang the basket by the loop from the hook.
6. Arrange the leaves of the plant so that they hang out and down
    from the basket. They will continue to grow this way.

To use the salad bowl, *you will need:*
a cheap, wooden salad bowl (you may paint it or leave it the
    natural wood color.)
three screws and a screwdriver (if you use a large bowl, you will
    need four screws.)
three (or four) lengths of strong ribbon, string, or brightly colored
    wool
large cup hook

1. Screw the three screws an equal distance apart into the sides of the bowl about ½ inch down from the top. Leave the heads of the screws sticking out.
2. Tie a length of string (or whatever you're using) *very securely* onto each of the screw heads.
3. Place your plant (in the pot) in the bowl.
4. Knot the string together at the top and make a little loop.
5. Screw the cup hook tightly into the window frame.
6. Arrange the plant leaves to trail down the sides of the bowl.
7. Hang the plant on the cup hook by the loop.

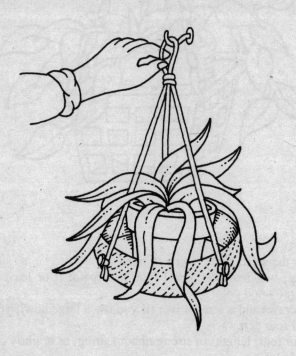

MAKE A CUTTING
OF A PLANT

You can make two or more plants from one original plant. Carefully clip a stalk or branch (not a leaf) from your selected houseplant. Place it in water in a window with good light. Add water every now and then to keep the water at the same level. The cutting should be at least halfway immersed in water.

In a week or two the cutting will begin to grow roots. When the roots are about 2 inches long and look sturdy, plant the new plant in a pot of healthy soil. Water it and place it in the light again.

Now you have two plants.

You can take several cuttings (not all at the same time) from one healthy plant.

CHAPTER 11

ALL KINDS OF PLANT PROJECTS

HOW TO
DYE
FLOWERS

You will need:

vegetable food coloring
freshly cut flowers
vase
water

1. Fill your vase with 1 inch of water. Put in enough vegetable dye to make the water very dark. Blue or green looks very pretty. You might also try red.
2. Slice the end of the stem of your chosen flower at an angle with a sharp knife. Carnations and lilies of the valley are good for this project.
3. Put your flower in the vase and watch it soak up the dye.
4. Very gradually the flower will begin to change color and in a few hours it will be the color you have chosen.

   This is also fun to do with celery stalks. Use a stalk with leaves and cut a slice or two off the bottom of the stalk. Place the stalk in a vase with 1 inch of water and coloring and in a few hours you will have very interesting looking celery. Since you are using vegetable dye, the celery is edible.

HOW TO DRY FLOWERS

You can pick wildflowers and dry them. Then you will have flowers all the year round. Pick the flowers on a dry day when blooms are at their fullest and most beautiful. Pick them in the morning after dew has dried or in the late afternoon. Dry only undamaged flowers. Flowers should be dried on the same day they are picked—strawflowers *must* be.

Here is a list of wildflowers that are good for drying and are easy to find. Some grow in the country, but others you may find growing wild in vacant city lots.

dock	celosia
goldenrod	lavender
joe-pye weed	pussy willow
cattail	yarrow
pampas grass	sunflower
milkweed pods	bachelor's button
baby's breath	Queen Anne's lace
blue salvia	

You can grow:
cockscomb
strawflowers
solotia

To dry flowers:
1. Cut plants while they are green.
2. Place them in a vase (or vaselike container) of water for about four hours.
3. Take them out of the water and strip off the leaves and any dead blooms very carefully.
4. Bunch them all together in small bunches of two or three plants. Tie up the stems. Don't damage the blooms.
5. Hang the bunch of flowers upside down in a dark, warm place where some air will circulate (like a closet with the door left ajar, for example) until they are dry.

MAKING
STRAWFLOWERS
TO LAST

You will need:
knife
fine, stiff wire cut into
lengths the size of
stems or size you want

1. Gather a bunch of buds and flowers.
2. Cut the stems off flowers.
3. Stick a length of wire into base of bloom.
4. When each flower has a wire stem, bunch them together and stand them upright in a container.
5. Place flowers outside in warm sun for a few hours to dry. If it's cold out or you haven't a good place outside, leave them in a dark place for about a week to dry. Strawflowers last a long time.

LEAF PRINTING

You will need:

> a small board
> piece of flannel or soft cloth
> piece of muslin
> rolling pin or wallpaper roller
>   (if using rolling pin, cover
>   with flannel)
> stamp ink pad
> newspapers
> watercolor paint brush
> different shaped leaves
> paper or cards for printing

1. Cover the board with flannel tightly.
2. Then cover over that with stretched muslin.
3. Brush the ink on the muslin but not to the edge.

4. Lay the leaf—vein side down—on the inked board.

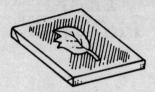

5. Cover the board with two pieces of newspaper.
6. Using a roller go back and forth over the board in the direction of the leaf. Use lots of pressure so that you get a good print.

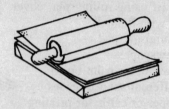

7. Remove newspaper and place inked leaf carefully, inked side down, on card or paper on which print is to be made.

8. Cover the leaf with paper and use roller as before.
9. Remove the paper and the leaf and let dry before handling.

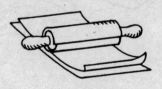

You can tell a tree's age by the rings inside the tree's trunk. Each year, unless it has been a very dry year, a tree grows a circle of light and dark wood. So if you count the rings you can tell approximately how old the tree is. Of course, you'd have to cut through the trunk to see the rings.

The Montezuma cypress in Tule, Mexico, is the widest-around tree in the world. Its circumference is 160 feet. That's very fat.

Paul: *What's it called when one tree listens in on another tree's conversation?*
Jonathan: *Leavesdropping?*

HOW TO MAKE
A
SPONGE GARDEN

You will need:

        a sponge
        a ribbon or cord
        shallow pan or
          dish of water
        grass seed or bird seed

1. Buy a natural sponge, not the kind that is man-made. You can get one at the hardware store or drug store.
2. Work a small hole through the center and thread a pretty ribbon or cord through the hole. Make a large knot at the bottom of the ribbon end so that the sponge won't slip off.

3. Sprinkle the grass seed or bird seed over the sponge.
4. Gently shake off the extra seed.

5. Dip the bottom of the sponge lightly in the pan of water and let the sponge soak up water. It should be wet but not dripping.

6. Hang the sponge in a sunny window.
7. Give it water each day by holding the pan underneath the sponge and letting it soak up water. Pretty soon when the seeds sprout you will have a very unusual hanging garden.

THINGS
TO MAKE
WITH SEEDS

SEED PICTURES

You can collect all kinds of seeds. There are melon seeds, cherry
seeds, grapefruit seeds, and lots of other seeds from your garden
and kitchen. Collect them and dry them. Or you can buy seeds.
Try to collect seeds of different sizes, shapes and colors.

You will need:

seeds
cardboard
white liquid glue
pencil

1. Draw a picture on the cardboard. Decide where you want to
   put the different seeds so that your picture is interesting and
   pleases you.
2. Spread the glue on the picture where you want the seeds.
3. Drop and sprinkle the seeds over the picture where the glue
   is spread. Most of the seeds will stick. You can press the
   seeds down to make sure they stick where you want them.
4. Shake off the excess seeds.

SEED JEWELRY

You can string together larger seeds with a needle and thick thread for necklaces and bracelets. Dip them in paints or vegetable dye to color them.

CHRISTMAS TREE DECORATIONS

String together large seeds or cranberries on strong thread with a needle and drape the chain on your tree.

HOW TO MAKE
A
SCARECROW

It would be funny to have a scarecrow in the middle of your garden to scare away the birds.

You will need:

an old string mop to use as the body
a piece of wood, a broom handle,
    for example, as the arms
heavy twine
an old dress or shirt
floppy old hat
about ten lengths of strips of
    rags or ribbon 12 inches long
something that will make noise
    when the breeze blows such
    as Chinese chimes or an old
    bell or whatever you can
    think of

1. Use the twine to tie the crosspiece (broom handle) to the mop stick near the mop end. This will be the arms. The mop end will be the hair of the scarecrow.
2. Slip the shirt or dress onto this, using the crosspiece as arms.

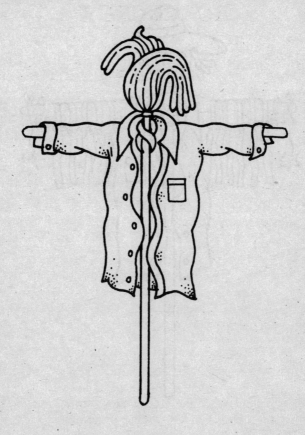

3. Tie the rag strips along the arms of the scarecrow so that they flutter in the breeze.

4. Tie the noisemaker to the end of the arms so that it will make noise when the wind blows.

5. Dig a hole about 10 inches deep in the middle of the garden and stick the end of your mop into the hole. Pack the earth tightly around the stick so that it won't fall over.
6. Put the hat on top of the mop, and that should scare anything.

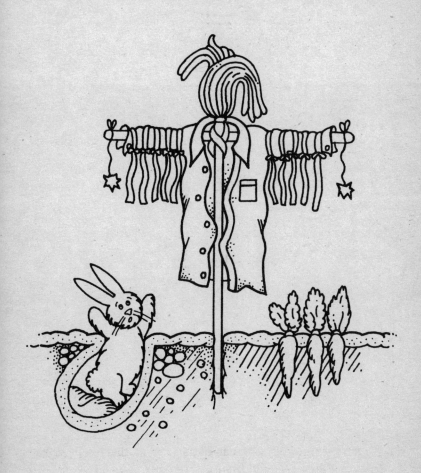